*A***FALCON**GUIDE®

Best Easy Day Hikes Series

Best Easy Day Hikes
Black Hills Country

Bert and Jane Gildart

D0483375

FALCONGUIDE®

GUILFORD, CONNECTICUT
HELENA, MONTANA

AN IMPRINT OF THE GLOBE PEQUOT PRESS

A **FALCON** GUICE ®□

Copyright © 2006 by Morris Book Publishing, LLC

Falcon and FalconGuide are registered trademarks of Morris Book Publishing, LLC.

Published in partnership with the Black Hills Parks and Forest Association.

Maps by David Sami, Multi Mapping LLC, and M.A. Dubé © 2006 by Morris Book Publishing LLC

Library of Congress Cataloging-in-Publication Data is available.

ISBN 0-7627-3544-9

Manufactured in the United States of America
First Edition/First Printing

To buy books in quantity for corporate use or incentives, call **(800) 962–0973, ext. 4551,** or e-mail **premiums@GlobePequot.com.**

Contents

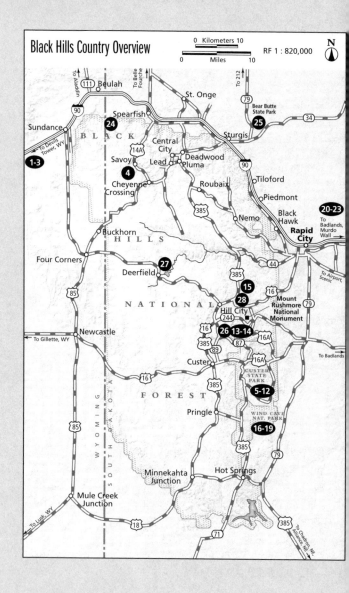

Black Hills Country Overview

0 Kilometers 10

0 Miles 10

RF 1 : 820,000

N

To Aladdin

111 Beulah

To Belle Fourche

St. Onge

Spearfish

To 212

79 Bear Butte State Park

34

Sundance

24

B L A C K

Sturgis

To Devils Tower, WY

1-3

14A

Central City

Savoy

Deadwood
Lead Pluma

90

Tiloford

4

Cheyenne Crossing

Roubaix

Piedmont

H I L L S

385 US

Nemo

Black Hawk

20-23
To Badlands, Murdo Wall

Buckhorn

Rapid City

Four Corners

27

44

To Airport, Scenic

Deerfield

N A T I O N A L

385

15

16

To Badlands

28

Mount Rushmore National Monument

85

Hill City

244

79

Newcastle

16

26 13-14

16A

To Gillette, WY

385

89

87

W Y O M I N G

Custer

16A

To Badlands

S O U T H   D A K O T A

F O R E S T

CUSTER STATE PARK

5-12

16

385

Pringle

WIND CAVE NAT. PARK

16-19

85

385

79

Minnekahta Junction

Hot Springs

Mule Creek Junction

To Lusk, WY

18

385

71

To Chadron, NE, Alliance, NE

Acknowledgments

Without the help of many people from the various agencies in the Black Hills, our work on this book would have been more difficult. No matter whom we contacted to verify information, we were greeted with friendliness, provided with appropriate suggestions, and presented with a willingness to take the time to review portions of the book for us.

We'd like to thank the following: Jim Jandreau, park manager of Bear Butte State Park; Christine Czazasty, chief of interpretation at Devils Tower National Monument; Marianne Mills, chief of resource education at Badlands National Park; Steve Baldwin, executive director of the Black Hills Parks and Forest Association; Craig Pugsley, visitor services coordinator of Custer State Park; Tom Farrell, chief of interpretation at Wind Cave National Park; Phyllis Cremonini, assistant chief of interpretation at Wind Cave National Park; Laura Burns from the USDA Forest Service, Hell Canyon Ranger District; the Forest Service for help with maps; and Gus Malon, Forest Service wilderness technician.

And last but not least, many thanks to Bill Schneider and Julie Marsh, our editors at The Globe Pequot Press.

All of you made the writing of this book go more easily.

Introduction

The Black Hills are a hiker's delight. Contained in these 6,000 square miles of unglaciated valleys and hills are more than 500 miles of trails that do great things. For one, they weave among incredible scenery sculpted by time in accordance with some of the nation's most provocative geological mandates. For another, they take you to splendid fishing. Wildlife abounds and roams freely (no bears, however!) in many areas. What all this boils down to is variety—something for everyone.

Once you begin to envision the area's immensity and the way in which it has affected travelers through the ages, including Crazy Horse, George Armstrong Custer, and a man named Colonel Dodge, you'll see why Dodge wrote, "The Black Hills country is a true oasis in a wide and dreary desert."

The hills' name was ascribed to them by the native people who first lived here and called them Paha Sapa, meaning "hills that are black." The color appears that way due to the predominance of ponderosa pine trees—the light and sun influence the overall effect of blackness produced by these trees.

Geologically, the land represents the easternmost extension of the Rocky Mountain uplift. The hills extend about 120 miles north to south and about 40 to 50 miles east to west. Outside of this area lie Badlands National Park, Devils Tower, and the Bearlodge Mountains in Wyoming—all created by the same forces as the Black Hills. Although divided politically, these areas are contiguous geographically, and we've kept them together for hikes in this book.

Best Easy Day Hikes Black Hills Country is an extrapolation of hikes from *Hiking the Black Hills Country*. We have endeavored to choose hikes that will appeal to all who visit this beautiful area, hikes that are easy enough to whet your appetite for something a bit longer and more strenuous. Realizing that "easy" for some is not easy for all, we hope to entice you onto the trails so that you get at least a brief overview of the riches of the Black Hills.

We have retained the hikes' geographic association throughout. Some sections contain short overviews to better acquaint you with the area. It's a good idea to use topographic and park maps and to realize your own limitations and heed them.

Practice zero-impact ethics as you hike. Then you and others who follow will have full enjoyment of the "hills."

Some Cautions and General Information

Weather in the Black Hills changes frequently and often without warning. Summer is one of the most pleasant times to be here, but lightning storms are frequent. Stay alert, get away from open ground and exposed ridges, and avoid single tall trees. Hypothermia is another possible risk. Cold rains often drench the mountains and you need to have the appropriate gear with you at all times to avoid getting soaked.

Although the water sources in the Black Hills look clean and enticing, do not drink from any water source unless you purify the water first. Fill your water bottles before setting out, making sure to carry enough to get you through the hike.

Nature runs wild all through the Black Hills. Encounters with free-roaming bison are often likely, and if this happens, move quietly away. No bears remain in the Black Hills, but a few mountain lions do. Lion attacks are rare and, truthfully, you'll be lucky if you see one. Mosquitoes are few, but poison ivy is abundant, especially along streams. Heed the adage, "Leaves of three, let it be." As in most woody areas, ticks can be another encounter of the personal kind. Use an insect repellent, and wear long pants and long-sleeved shirts. Rattlesnakes are common in the Black Hills, especially around prairie-dog communities. Most will avoid you; just watch where you sit and step.

As you walk, remember that much of the region is a "multiple-use area," meaning that you might share a trail with bikers and horse riders. If stock is encountered, you should move quietly to the down side of the trail to let them pass.

Getting there: In South Dakota take Interstate 90 (I-90) from the east or west; U.S. Highway 385, 85, or 79 from the north or south; or U.S. Highway 16 or 34 from the east or west to the Black Hills and enter from any number of signposted locations.

Camping and contacts: National Park, Forest Service, and private campgrounds are as abundant as the trees throughout the Black Hills. They range from those with facilities to more primitive options. Some require reservations, and those near or on lakes and those with showers seem to fill the fastest. For reservations in Custer State Park, call (800) 710-2267; for sites in the Black Hills National Forest, call (800) 280-2267. Several good Web sites cover nearly all you'll want to know. Access www.theblackhills.com, www.black hillsinfo.com, www.fs.fed.us/r2/blackhills, and www.bad lands.national-park.com.

A South Dakota fishing license is required for fishing in all lakes and streams in that state.

Suggested Hiker's List

Good-quality rain gear
A light and warm jacket
Sweater
Long pants
Shorts
Long and short-sleeve shirts
Comfortable hiking boots
Hats: one with sun visor, one wool
Water (take plenty)
Insect repellent and sunscreen
Your camera
Snacks and a plastic bag for trash
Map(s) and your FalconGuide

Ranking the Hikes

Although the hikes in this book are relatively easy, some are longer and have more elevation changes than others. Here's a list of the hikes in order of difficulty, from easiest to more challenging.

20   Door Trail, Badlands National Park
21   Window Trail, Badlands National Park
 1   Tower Trail, Devils Tower National Monument
 8   Creekside Trail, Custer State Park
 5   Sylvan Lake Shore Trail, Custer State Park
 2   Red Beds Trail, Devils Tower National Monument
 3   Joyner Ridge Trail, Devils Tower National Monument
10   Badger Clark Historic Trail, Custer State Park
16   Garden of Eden Cave Tour, Wind Cave National Park

Hike/Bike Trails

Map Legend

Boundaries

National park boundary	/////////
Other Park/Forest	⟋⟍⟋⟍⟋

Transportation

Interstate highway	〔40〕
U.S. highway	〔89〕
State highway	〔64〕
Other highway	〔18〕〔610〕
Primary/other roads	————
Unpaved road	————
Unimproved road	= = = = =
Featured trail	▬▬▬▬
Shared trail	••••••••••
Other trail	- - - - - -

Hydrology

River	
Creek	
Intermittent stream	
Spring	⌐ρ
Falls/rapids	∥
Lake	
Sand	

Physiography

Cliff	⌢⌢⌢⌢
Pass	)(
Peak/elevation	▲+ Dickey Hill 2,444 ft.

Symbols

Amphitheater	◖
Bridge	≍
Backcountry campsite	▲
Cabin/shelter	⌂
Campground	△
Lodge	⌂
Gate	•—•
Turnaround	↻
Overlook	◉
Parking	🅿
Picnic area	🛆
Point of interest	▪
Park entrance	🚻 ▸
Restroom	🚻
Town	○
Trailhead	🚶
Visitor center	❓
Wildlife area	➤

Hikes in Wyoming

Devils Tower National Monument

Devils Tower rises 867 feet from its base, 1,267 feet above the Belle Fourche River, and 5,117 feet above sea level. Because of its imposing nature and its stable rock, over 4,000 climbers attempt to scale its heights each year, and at least 200 routes have so far been established. Devils Tower rises spectacularly in northeast Wyoming and is our nation's first national monument.

Because Native Americans have long revered the monolith, in recent years some shift in management has occurred. Today, in addition to its status as a national monument, Devils Tower is managed for its spiritual significance, a decision appreciated by Native Americans. Devils Tower is sacred to twenty-three tribes. Native Americans have prayed here for thousands of years before the tower was first climbed on July 4, 1893, with the aid of a ladder. Today signs near the tower remind visitors not to disturb prayer flags and bundles. There is a voluntary climbing closure in the month of June to respect the religious practices of the Native Americans during that period. Some routes are closed from mid-March to summer to protect nesting falcons.

Although many come here to scale Devils Tower, the landscape surrounding the tower should not go unnoticed. The Park Service lists five trails at the monument, totaling nearly 8 miles. We've included three here, which most of you can complete in the course of an hour. But the challenge is not completing the hikes—for these are truly easy—rather the challenge is in not becoming so absorbed by the tower's grandeur that you lose all track of time.

Devils Tower is 27 miles northwest of Sundance, Wyoming, along U.S. Highway 14 and Wyoming Highway 24 and 107 miles west and north of Rapid City, South Dakota. Take Interstate 90 west from Rapid City for 80 miles to US 14, then head north for 21 miles to WY 24. Go north on WY 24 for 6 miles to the entrance gate.

1 Tower Trail

A walk through millions of years of the earth's past as well as more recent human history.

Start: From the trailhead at the visitor center.
Distance: 1.25-mile loop.
Approximate hiking time: 1 to 1½ hours.
Difficulty: A relatively flat, easy circuit trail.
Seasons: Best from spring through fall.

Maps: Free trail brochure with map, available at entrance gate and visitor center.
Trail contact: Devils Tower National Monument, Box 8, Devils Tower, WY 82714, (307) 467-5283.

Finding the trailhead: The trail begins at the visitor center, which is 3 miles from the entrance gate.

The Hike

The Tower Trail is perhaps the most popular area trail because it most closely rings the base of Devils Tower, and it provides hikers with an almost bird's-eye view of climbers as they scale the vertical columns. The path wanders through boulder fields and passes through stands of ponderosa pine, typical of other Black Hills vegetation. The trail also approaches columns that have sloughed off over the millennia and which, in turn, have been modified by the weather. Geologically, this trail excites those with a scientific bent and stirs the imagination in all who hike here. Along the way the park provides benches and interpretive signs. About midway the park provides a mounted set of viewing binoculars. The

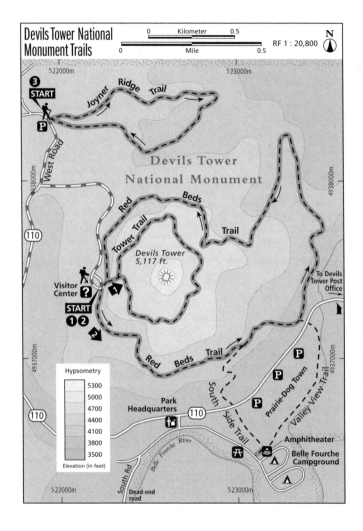

Devils Tower National Monument Trails

Kilometer		
0		0.5
0	Mile	0.5

RF 1 : 20,800

N

3 START

P

Joyner Ridge Trail

West Road

522000m

523000m

4938000m

Devils Tower National Monument

Red Beds Trail

Tower Trail

Devils Tower 5,117 ft.

Visitor Center ?

START 1 2

1

2

Red Beds Trail

110

To Devils Tower Post Office

4937000m

P

P

P

Prairie-Dog Town

Valley View Trail

South Side Trail

Hypsometry	
	5300
	5000
	4700
	4400
	4100
	3800
	3500
Elevation (in feet)	

Park Headquarters

110

Belle Fourche River

Amphitheater

Belle Fourche Campground

South Rd

Dead-end road

522000m

523000m

entire trail is paved though is somewhat bumpy. On the southeast side a viewing tube focuses on the remains of the old ladder used in 1893 for the first climb. Pigeons and rock doves wing along the columns, and vultures often mass near the top.

2 Red Beds Trail

A longer trail than the Tower Trail, this one encircles Devils Tower from a greater distance and perspective.

See map on page 10.
Start: From the visitor center.
Distance: 2.8-mile loop.
Approximate hiking time: 2 to 3 hours.
Difficulty: Easy to moderate.
Seasons: Best from May through fall.

Maps: Free trail brochure with map, available at entrance gate and visitor center.
Trail contact: Devils Tower National Monument, Box 8, Devils Tower, WY 82714, (307) 467-5283.

Finding the trailhead: The trail can be accessed from the visitor center or from one of the park's other trails that depart from the campground located about 0.5 mile from the entrance station.

The Hike

The Red Beds Trail also rings Devils Tower, but from a greater distance. Beginning at the visitor center and proceeding south (counterclockwise), the trail descends slightly. Rock formations soon obscure Devils Tower. At 0.7 mile the trail skirts a prairie-dog community and then lives up to its name as it passes through formations of red rocks (the red beds). In another 0.5 mile the trail parallels the Belle Fourche River, then ascends several hundred feet, where it once again approaches Devils Tower.

Miles and Directions

0.0 Begin at the visitor center.

0.7 The trail skirts a prairie-dog town.

1.2 The trail parallels the Belle Fourche River.

2.8 The trail ends.

3 Joyner Ridge Trail

This trek will take you through three major Devils Tower ecosystems.

See map on page 10.
Start: From the trailhead on West Road in the monument.
Distance: 1.5-mile loop.
Approximate hiking time: 1 to 2 hours.
Difficulty: Easy to moderate.
Seasons: Late April or May through October.
Maps: Free trail brochure and map available at entrance gate and visitor center.
Trail contact: Devils Tower National Monument, Box 8, Devils Tower, WY 82714, (307) 467–5283.

Finding the trailhead: Access this trail by following the park road from the entrance station for 2 miles until it intersects with West Road on your left. Take West Road 0.5 mile to the trailhead.

The Hike

Joyner Ridge trail is a 1.5-mile loop that is most easily hiked in a clockwise direction. This hike provides more distant perspectives of Devils Tower while simultaneously providing stunning views of the monument's three major ecosystems. These include the prairie, riparian, and ponderosa-pine habitats. Deer abound throughout. Signs along the way interpret the communities and enhance nature's abundant manifestations. Keep alert for prairie rattlesnakes.

Hikes in South Dakota
Spearfish Area

The Spearfish Canyon area is so special that a National Scenic Byway of more than 18 miles winds through the canyon walls and tree-covered slopes, providing a tour of unparalleled beauty. Hikers would be wise to drive this road, as it serves to give an excellent overview of this section of the Black Hills, which is managed as part of Black Hills National Forest.

The wonderful geological formations in the canyon began to take shape thirty million to sixty million years ago. Three types of rock dominate: The oldest is Paha limestone, then the red hue of Englewood limestone, and finally, the brown Deadwood shale.

Botanically, four distinctly different vegetative regions thrive in the canyon, which in itself is unusual. Here then, is a meeting place for plants, trees, and bushes from the Great Plains, from the Rocky Mountains, and from the Eastern deciduous and Northern forests. No clear explanation exists for their diversity, though it probably derives from ancient climatic changes. Another novelty, it is said, is that Spearfish Creek is the only known river in the region to freeze from the bottom up.

Several trails exist in Spearfish Canyon, and each provides both beauty and tranquility.

4 Rimrock Trail Lower Loop

A loop hike through large stands of ponderosa, aspen, and birch, with a gradual descent into Little Spearfish Canyon.

Start: Trailhead at the west end of the Rod and Gun Campground on Forest Road 222.
Distance: 3.5-mile loop.
Approximate hiking time: 2 to 4 hours.
Difficulty: Easy to moderately easy.
Seasons: Late spring through fall.
Maps: Black Hills National Forest Map; Rimrock Trail No. 79

Map; Black Hills National Forest handout available free from Forest Service offices, trailhead boxes, and visitor centers.
Trail contacts: Northern Hills Ranger District, 2014 North Main, Spearfish, SD 57783, (605) 642–4622; Black Hills National Forest Supervisor's Office and Visitor Center, RR2, Box 200, Custer, SD 57730, (605) 673–2251.

Finding the trailhead: Take U.S. Highway 14A (Spearfish Canyon National Scenic Byway) south from Spearfish for 12.8 miles to Savoy. Then take FR 222 south for about 6 miles to the Rod and Gun Campground. The trailhead is on the west end of the campground.

The Hike

The Lower Loop is the shorter of the two loop trails here. To take this route, begin your hike at the west end of the Rod and Gun Campground. The trail passes through a cattle gate and then immediately ascends for about 0.8 mile to the rim of the canyon, in a westerly direction. It then levels out through ponderosa pine, quaking aspen, and stands of birch for about 0.5 mile. Deer tracks abound, and flickers

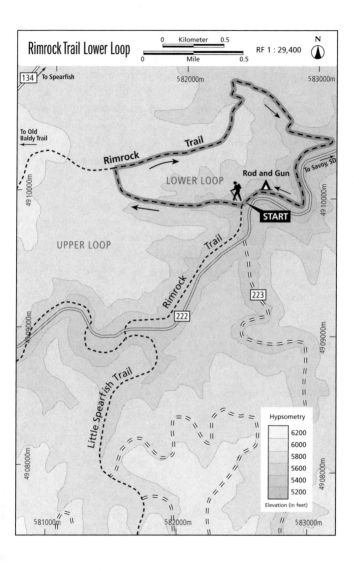

Rimrock Trail Lower Loop

| 0 | Kilometer | 0.5 |

| 0 | Mile | 0.5 |

RF 1 : 29,400

N

134 To Spearfish

582000m

583000m

To Old
Baldy Trail

Rimrock   Trail

LOWER LOOP

Rod and Gun

To Savoy, SD

49 10000m

49 10000m

START

UPPER LOOP

Rimrock   Trail

223

49 09000m

49 09000m

49 09000m

222

Little Spearfish Trail

Hypsometry	
	6200
	6000
	5800
	5600
	5400
	5200

Elevation (in feet)

49 08000m

49 08000m

581000m

582000m

583000m

dart among the tree branches. The variation and abundance of plant life in this area are amazing and include juniper, sage, varied wildflowers, buck brush, and kinnikinnick, a favorite grouse dish. The remainder of the trail gradually descends into the depths of Little Spearfish Canyon, where the rock walls and formations stand in mute testimony to the forces of nature. A brief hike through tall grasses returns hikers to the trailhead.

The loops of the Rimrock Trail are designed for hikers, horsebackers, and mountain bikers. Horse use appears light, with no evidence of trail erosion.

Miles and Directions

0.0 Begin at the trailhead for the lower loop.
0.8 The trail ascends to the canyon rim.
1.0 At the T intersection go right (east).
3.5 Return to the trailhead.

Honorable Mention

Roughlock Falls

The Savoy area is a popular one for several reasons. Here, two huge canyons, Spearfish and Little Spearfish, come together to offer spectacular views. The ancient rock formations are a geologist's delight. And Little Spearfish Canyon offers wonderful hiking trails and fishing spots.

The trail to Roughlock Falls is a flat, easy, 1-mile walk along Spearfish Creek to the picturesque waterfall, which is a favorite picnic spot. The trail is wide and barrier-free, accessible to visitors in wheelchairs. The cascading falls are charming at all times of the year. The falls are so named because, before the current road existed, the old wagon and log-sled path was very steep. Drivers "rough-locked" the wheels of their vehicles with ropes or chains so the wagons would drag instead of jacking out of control.

Roughlock Falls is located about 0.5 mile from Savoy on Forest Hill Road 222. To reach Savoy, take U.S. Highway 14A (Spearfish Canyon National Scenic Byway) south from Spearfish for 12.8 miles. Just south of Savoy, find a parking area on your left. From here, you can hike a wide, tree-lined path for 1 mile along Spearfish Creek to Roughlock Falls.

Hikes in South Dakota

Custer State Park

Custer State Park consists of grasslands, ponderosa-pine forests, bur oak, and white spruce. As a wildlife preserve, Custer has one of the world's largest bison herds and is home to elk, deer, bighorn sheep, and even mountain goats. At 71,000 acres it is one of the largest state parks in our nation.

The park is located in the southeast portion of the Black Hills, directly north of Wind Cave National Park and about a thirty-minute drive south from Rapid City, South Dakota. From Interstate 90 at Rapid City, take South Dakota Highway 79 south for 17 miles. About 1 mile south of Hermosa, follow South Dakota Highway 36 west for 9 miles to U.S. Highway 16A west and to the park's east entrance. The Peter Norbeck Visitor Center is located on US 16A about 3 miles west of the junction of SD 36 and US 16; it is open from April through November. The Wildlife Station Visitor Center, located on the east side of the Wildlife Loop Road, is open from the end of May through September. A small day-use fee is charged.

Though the trail system is not extensive, it is varied. Trails in Custer State Park wind through prairies, mountains, and incredible rock formations. They offer abundant views of wildlife, lakes, and streams. They're varied enough to let you hear the insects, to see the abundant wildlife, and to allow the winds to shape your thoughts.

5 Sylvan Lake Shore Trail

An interpretive trail with wonderful views.

Start: From the Sylvan Lake Day-Use area.
Distance: 1-mile loop.
Approximate hiking time: 1 to 1 1/2 hours.
Difficulty: Easy, mostly barrier-free.
Seasons: Best from May through October.
Fees and permits: Custer State

Park entry permit required.
Maps: National Geographic/ Trails Illustrated Topo Map No. 238; Free Custer State Park Trail Guide available at park office, visitor centers, and entrance stations.
Trail contact: Custer State Park, HC 83, Box 70, Custer, SD 57730, (605) 255-4515.

Finding the trailhead: From Peter Norbeck Visitor Center, take U.S. Highway 16A west to South Dakota Highway 87 north (Needles Highway) then west to Sylvan Lake Day-Use area, a total of 19 miles.

The Hike

The interpretive Sylvan Lake Shore Trail is one of the easiest in Custer State Park. This trail makes a loop around the lake, affording walkers wonderful views of the gigantic granite rocks in and around the lake. This extremely easy walk is for everyone. The majority of the trail is barrier-free.

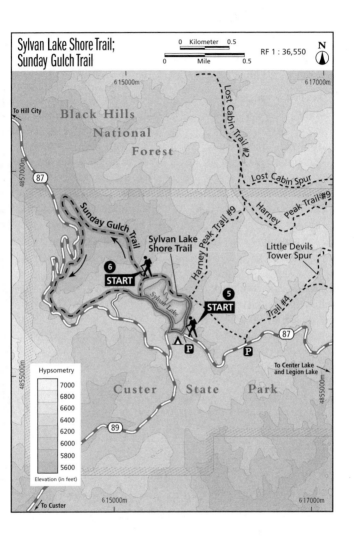

**Sylvan Lake Shore Trail;
Sunday Gulch Trail**

0   Kilometer   0.5

0   Mile   0.5

RF 1 : 36,550

N

Black Hills

National

Forest

To Hill City

Lost Cabin Trail #2

Lost Cabin Spur

Harney Peak Trail #9

Harney Peak Trail #9

Sunday Gulch Trail

**Sylvan Lake
Shore Trail**

Little Devils
Tower Spur

**6
START**

Sylvan Lake

**5
START**

Trail #4

87

To Center Lake
and Legion Lake

Hypsometry

	7000
	6800
	6600
	6400
	6200
	6000
	5800
	5600

Elevation (in feet)

Custer   State   Park

89

To Custer

6 Sunday Gulch Trail

A unique trail, one of beauty; a National Recreation Trail.

See map on page 23.
Start: From the Sylvan Lake Shore Trail at Sylvan Lake.
Distance: 2.8-mile loop.
Approximate hiking time: 3 to 4 hours.
Difficulty: Moderate.
Seasons: From June through October.
Fees and permits: Custer State

Park entry permit required.
Maps: National Geographic/ Trails Illustrated Topo Map No. 238; Custer State Park Trail Guide booklet available at park office, visitor centers, and entrances.
Trail contact: Custer State Park, HC 83, Box 70, Custer, SD 57730, (605) 255–4515.

Finding the trailhead: From Peter Norbeck Visitor Center, take U.S. Highway 16A west, then take South Dakota Highway 87 north then west to Sylvan Lake, a total distance of 18.8 miles. Park in the day-use parking lot. Walk the Sylvan Lake Shore Trail east for 0.25 mile to the trailhead sign on the left. Or come in at the Sylvan Lake entrance station via US 16/385 south from Hill City to SD 87 south to Sylvan Lake.

From Custer, take South Dakota Highway 89 north for approximately 7 miles to Sylvan Lake.

The Hike

The Sunday Gulch Trail is considered so extraordinary in the spectrum of plants, trees, mosses, and scenery that, in 1971, it was designated a National Recreation Trail. Hike this trail counterclockwise, starting off to the northwest. This beautiful trail immediately descends steeply for 0.25 mile, winding over huge rocks as it drops into the depths of Sunday Gulch. Because the rocks can be slippery for the first portion of the hike, the park has provided some stone steps and handrails. Exercise caution on this part of the descent, since winter ice pushing on the railing can sometimes loosen the handrails.

As you begin the descent, huge granite walls tower on each side of the trail, which parallels the creek as it drops into the ravine. Various rock layers and formations exist here. Tiny waterfalls and rock grottos surrounded by ponderosa pine, Black Hills spruce *(Picea glauca* var. *densata)*, paper birch, and aspen provide numerous photo opportunities. Old man's beard, a gray-green lichen, hangs from the trees, adding to the mysterious aura of the gulch. Many of the rocks are covered with mosses and lichen. Once this gulch was filled with a stream, but in the 1890s Theodor Reder dammed the mouth of the gulch and created Sylvan Lake. Today the stream spills over the dam, and at least one deep pool provides a home to brown trout.

As the trail ascends from the gulch, beautiful panoramas of the Needles formations slide into view. Toward trail's end hikers encounter a power line, and at times the trail parallels the road; still, the beauty of the area is not diminished. The trail is well marked with orange blazes on trees.

7 Grace Coolidge Walk-in Fishing Area

A beautiful, fairly flat walk terminating or beginning at Center Lake or Grace Coolidge Campground that parallels (with many crossings) Grace Coolidge Creek.

Start: Begin at Grace Coolidge Campground or Center Lake.
Distance: 5.6 miles out and back.
Approximate hiking time: 5 to 6 hours.
Difficulty: Easy.
Seasons: Best in spring through fall.
Fees and permits: Custer State Park entry permit required.

Maps: National Geographic/ Trails Illustrated Topo Map No. 238; Custer State Park Trail Guide available at visitor centers, park office, and entrance stations.
Trail contact: Custer State Park, HC 83, Box 70, Custer, SD 57730, (605) 255-4515.

Finding the trailhead: For the southern trailhead, take U.S. Highway 16A west from Peter Norbeck Visitor Center for 1.5 miles. The trailhead is on the right, across the road from the Grace Coolidge Campground. To access the northern trailhead, take US 16A west from Peter Norbeck Visitor Center to South Dakota Highway 87 north to the turnoff for Center Lake and the Black Hills Playhouse, a total of 8 miles. Go in 1 mile to Center Lake. The trailhead is located by the shower house above the lake.

The Hike

The Grace Coolidge Walk-in Fishing Area trail is actually an old, overgrown logging road. It is an easy and refreshing hike, and the numerous crossings over the narrow, sometimes

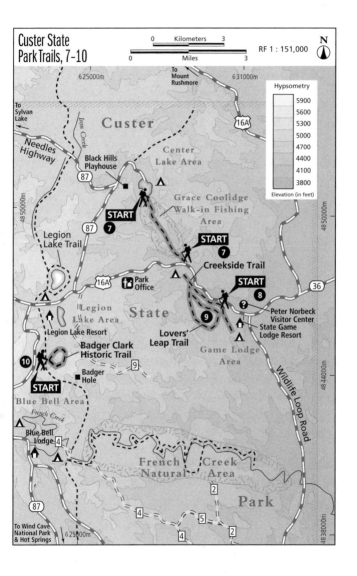

Custer State Park Trails, 7–10

Kilometers 3
Miles 3

RF 1 : 151,000

N

Hypsometry

| 5900 |
| 5600 |
| 5300 |
| 5000 |
| 4700 |
| 4400 |
| 4100 |
| 3800 |

Elevation (in feet)

To Mount Rushmore

To Sylvan Lake

Needles Highway

Iron Creek

Custer

16A

Black Hills Playhouse

87

Center Lake Area

Grace Coolidge Walk-in Fishing Area

START 7

Legion Lake Trail

87

START 7

Creekside Trail

16A

Park Office

START 8

?

Peter Norbeck Visitor Center

State Game Lodge Resort

36

Legion Lake Area

State

9

Legion Lake Resort

Lovers' Leap Trail

Badger Clark Historic Trail

9

Game Lodge Area

10

Badger Hole

START

Blue Bell Area

French Creek

Wildlife Loop Road

Blue Bell Lodge 4

French Creek Natural Area

Park

87

To Wind Cave National Park & Hot Springs

625000m

4

5

2

2

deep, creek add to the fun. Six lowhead dams exist along the way, some with deep dark pools lying beneath granite rock formations. Walking this trail is a fun outing for the entire family.

In the summer the trail is alive with the vibrant colors of wildflowers; in the fall the bur oak and birch tree leaves add a startling gold that contrasts with the green-black of the ponderosa pine. As in many low, wet areas, poison ivy is abundant along the trail and by the creek.

Photo opportunities abound here, as do chances for excellent fishing. The pools are stocked with rainbow and brook trout, so hiking anglers should be sure to pack in fishing gear along with their South Dakota license.

In 1927 President Calvin Coolidge and his family maintained a summer White House nearby; as a result, many features in the area bear the Coolidge name.

8 Creekside Trail

A beautiful stroll on a multi-accessible hard-surface path, which parallels Grace Coolidge Creek.

See map on page 27.
Start: From either end or any-place along the trail.
Distance: 2 miles one-way.

Approximate hiking time: 1 to 2 hours.
Difficulty: Easy.
Fees and permits: Custer State Park entry permit required.

Finding the trailhead: Begin at the State Game Lodge Campground or at Grace Coolidge Campground. The trail runs between them paralleling Grace Coolidge Creek.

The Hike

This trail offers a new dimension for all visitors in that it is wheelchair accessible, easily walked, and safe for energetic children. The trail is open to hiking, biking, and in-line skating. This newly established trail follows Grace Coolidge Creek and passes by the historic State Game Lodge, the Peter Norbeck Visitor Center, Coolidge General Store, and the park office. Visitors may access the trail at any of these locations. Also, if you begin at the State Game Lodge Campground and have energy and time left over, you can keep on hiking into the Grace Coolidge Walk-in Fishing Area.

9 Lovers' Leap Trail

A loop hike that's a great family outing, with some ups and downs, a few stream crossings, and many wonderful views.

See map on page 27.
Start: At the trailhead behind the schoolhouse across from Peter Norbeck Visitor Center.
Distance: 3-mile loop.
Approximate hiking time: 2 to 4 hours.
Difficulty: Moderately strenuous; the trail becomes moderate to easy after the first 30 minutes.
Elevation gain: 480 feet.
Highest elevation: 4,780 feet.
Seasons: Best from late spring through fall.
Fees and permits: Custer State Park entry permit permit.
Maps: National Geographic/ Trails Illustrated Topo Map No. 238; Custer State Park Trail Guide booklet available at the park office, visitor centers, and entrances.
Trail contact: Custer State Park, HC 83, Box 70, Custer, SD 57730, (605) 255-4515.

Finding the trailhead: The trail begins behind the schoolhouse across from the Peter Norbeck Visitor Center on U.S. Highway 16A, which is 3 miles east of the park entrance station off South Dakota Highway 36.

The Hike

With lots of potential for a fun family outing, this hike combines gentle ups and downs after an initial steep ascent to a ridge. Numerous stream crossings exist here, though none is too difficult. Poison ivy can be abundant along the streams.

According to legend, Lovers' Leap derives its name from a Native American couple who elected to end their lives by plummeting from the lofty outcropping of rocks on a 200-foot ridge. Just why the couple leaped to their deaths is not certain. Today a lone ponderosa pine stands among the conglomerate rocks overlooking the sheer drop of several hundred feet. Not surprisingly, the ridge commands spectacular views of the Black Hills.

The overlook is reached by following the broad trail from the schoolhouse, where it immediately begins a thirty- to forty-five-minute, relatively steep climb through bur oak and ponderosa-pine forest. Near the top, prairie grasses mat the hillsides. As you approach the summit, interesting rock formations and lichen-covered boulders are scattered on the hill to your right. The trail begins to level out as you near the site of Lovers' Leap.

At the trail's highest point, a sign greets you and provides the following message: "Custer State Park is a place where one can still be an unworried and unregimented individual and wear any old clothes and sit on a log and get his sanity back again." Beyond the trail and sign, hikers can climb the short distance through the boulders and reach the deadly point from which the lovers once leapt.

The view from the summit (elevation 4,780 feet) is spectacular. Across the valley and in the near distance are the charred remains of the Galena Fire of 1988. Looking beyond, on clear days, hikers are treated to a view of Harney Peak, Mount Coolidge, and the Cathedral Spires.

Upon leaving Lovers' Leap, the trail descends the west side of the ridge to Galena Creek, and here hikers may experience some difficulty. The trail meanders along the narrow creek bed and makes ten stream crossings. In dry times crossing is easy, but in wet years the water remains high. Poison ivy abounds along the creek bed and the trail, so wear long pants and watch where you place your feet. Much of the trail is flanked with less irritating, lovelier wildflowers such as sedum, highbush cranberry, cow parsnip, Bicknell's geranium, mountain meadowsweet, bluebells, salsify, and many prairie grasses.

After the last stream crossing, the trail leads to the road and passes by the Coolidge Inn. A ten-minute walk will return you to the schoolhouse and the trailhead.

Miles and Directions

- **0.0** Begin at the trailhead.
- **2.0** Arrive at Lovers' Leap Overlook.
- **2.5** A series of stream crossings begins.
- **3.0** Return to the trailhead.

10 Badger Clark Historic Trail

A walk back in history, one that's great for the whole family. You'll get to visit the historic cabin of the first poet laureate of South Dakota.

See map on page 27.
Start: From the trailhead at Badger Hole Drive, 6.5 miles from Peter Norbeck Visitor Center.
Distance: 1-mile loop.
Approximate hiking time: 1 to 2 hours.
Difficulty: Moderately easy.
Seasons: Best from late spring through fall.

Fees and permits: Custer State Park entry permit required.
Maps: Free Custer State Park Trail Guide and interpretive booklet available at park office, visitor centers, and entrance stations.
Trail contact: Custer State Park, HC 83, Box 70, Custer, SD 57730, (605) 255-4515.

Finding the trailhead: From the Peter Norbeck Visitor Center, take U.S. Highway 16A west for 5.5 miles to the sign on the left for the Badger Hole (Park Road 9). Follow this road for 1 mile to Badger Hole Drive on the right. Turn right and go less than 0.1 mile to the trailhead parking lot.

The Hike

There's a song in the canyon below me / And a song in the pines overhead, / As the sunlight crawls down from the snowline / And rustles the deer from his bed. / With mountains of green all around me / And mountains of white up above / And mountains of blue down the ski-line, / I follow the trail that I love.

—Badger Clark, in *The Old Prospector in Sun and Saddle Leather*

This short, historic interpretive walk is great for the entire family. The well-marked trail exists because the area was once the haunt of poet Badger Clark (1883–1957), best known perhaps for his poem "Cowboy's Prayer." Clark lived alone for thirty years in this pristine setting, inspired by nature's bounty. He first built a one-room cabin, where he lived for ten years while building a slightly larger cabin just up the hill. An interpretive trail brochure tells more about Clark's life and is available at the cabin and the park's visitor centers.

The trail begins with a moderate ascent clockwise through pine. At about 0.5 mile hikers can see the charred remains of the Galena Fire of 1988 and the lookout tower atop Mount Coolidge (6,023 feet). Note the large rocks placed along the trail as it ascends to the vista. According to the interpretive brochure, this was the area where Clark originally wanted to be buried, and so he began lining the path with rocks. He often traveled this path, which provided inspiration for his work.

Custer State Park has provided ten stops along the trail, with poetry selections to be read from the brochure at each stop. You will note that one of the three Centennial Trail trailheads in Custer State Park is located near this place known as the "Badger Hole."

11 French Creek Natural Area

This trip in its entirety is long (12 miles), and many trekkers often camp for one night. Therefore, we suggest making this a trip of only 1.5 miles one-way. The trail is marked from both the east and west terminuses for this length; after that, hikers must make their own way. The trip travels along a gorge of unique rock formations, intersected by many stream crossings.

Start: From the trailhead on the Wildlife Loop Road.
Distance: 3 miles out and back.
Approximate hiking time: 2 hours.
Difficulty: Easy to moderate.
Other trail users: Horseback riders.
Seasons: Best from late spring through fall.

Fees and permits: Custer State Park entry permit required.
Maps: National Geographic/ Trails Illustrated Topo Map No. 238; free Custer State Park Trail Guide.
Trail contact: Custer State Park, HC 83, Box 70, Custer, SD 57730, (605) 255-4515.

Finding the trailhead: To reach the east trailhead, go east from Peter Norbeck Visitor Center on U.S. Highway 16A for 0.8 mile to the Wildlife Loop Road, on the right. Turn and follow this road south for 4 miles to the trailhead sign on the right.

The Hike

French Creek originates northwest of the town of Custer and travels east through Custer State Park in a dramatic manner, exposing layers of ancient rock in colorful canyons. Near here one of Lt. Col. George Custer's men discovered gold in 1874.

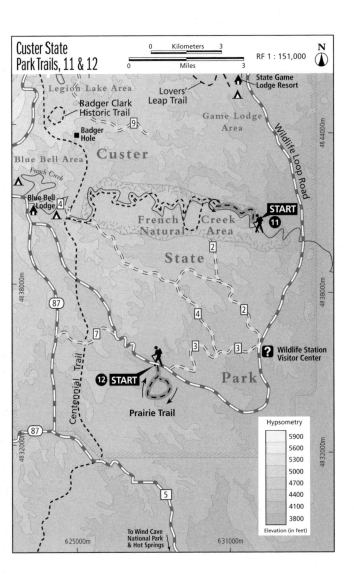

Custer State
Park Trails, 11 & 12

RF 1 : 151,000

N

Kilometers 3

Miles 3

Legion Lake Area

Lovers' Leap Trail

State Game Lodge Resort

Badger Clark Historic Trail

Game Lodge Area

Badger Hole

9

Custer

Blue Bell Area

French Creek

Blue Bell Lodge

4

French Creek Natural Area

START 11

2

State

Wildlife Loop Road

48 44000m

48 38000m

2

87

4

2

7

Centennial Trail

3

3

Wildlife Station Visitor Center

12 START

Park

Prairie Trail

87

48 32000m

48 32000m

5

To Wind Cave National Park & Hot Springs

625000m

631000m

Hypsometry

	5900
	5600
	5300
	5000
	4700
	4400
	4100
	3800

Elevation (in feet)

Fishing here (you must have a state license) is good for brown and rainbow trout. Wildlife is here, too, as well as an amazing geological phenomenon. Near the east end of the trail, the waters of French Creek disappear for several hundred yards, providing an excellent example of "sinkhole" topography.

The trail is easy to follow; if you do not turn around after the first 1.5 miles, then you are often on your own to make a trail, which is fairly easy to do by just following the stream. Watch for snakes and poison ivy.

If you should decide to hike in and stay overnight, you may camp anywhere along the trail. Park rules prohibit open fires in this area.

Miles and Directions

0.0 Start the trail at the eastern terminus.

1.0 The stream disappears.

1.5 This is the suggested turnaround point.

3.0 Return to the east trailhead.

12 Prairie Trail

An interpretive loop hike through prairie grasslands and over open ridges with superb views.

See map on page 35.
Start: From the trailhead on the Wildlife Loop Road, about 15 miles from the Peter Norbeck Visitor Center.
Distance: 3-mile lollipop.
Approximate hiking time: 2 to 3 hours.
Difficulty: Easy.
Seasons: Best from spring through fall.

Fees and permits: Custer State Park entry permit required.
Maps: National Geographic/ Trails Illustrated Topo Map No. 238; Custer State Park Trail Guide available at park office, visitor centers, and entrance stations.
Trail contact: Custer State Park, HC 83, Box 70, Custer, SD 57730, (605) 255-4515.

Finding the trailhead: From the Peter Norbeck Visitor Center on U.S. Highway 16A, go east for 0.8 mile to the Wildlife Loop Road intersecting from the south. Take a right onto the Loop road for approximately 14 miles. The well-marked trailhead is on the left, and offers a small parking area. From the Blue Bell entrance station on South Dakota Highway 87, take the Wildlife Loop Road southeast for 5 miles to the trailhead on the right.

The Hike

The Prairie Trail was designed especially for those interested in viewing prairie grasslands and wildflowers. The interpretive signs help ensure more correct interpretation and add to the enjoyment of the hike. The elevation gain is modest and climbs but 250 feet.

Views offered along this trail are commanding, and on a clear day hikers are rewarded with distant views to the east of the White River Badlands. Even from afar, when the interplay of light and land is appropriate, the area appears majestic. So, too, does the grassland over which hikers must pass. Views of the prairie suggest an immensity and grandeur found in few other areas of the United States. The flora is varied, and throughout the summer, pageants of flowers reward hikers. Alert travelers might also see and hear a variety of birds and mammals, such as mountain bluebirds, golden eagles, coyotes, and pronghorns.

The Prairie Trail begins by immediately crossing the narrow South Fork of Lame Johnny Creek, which, following rains, generally means wet feet. The path meanders through the grassland for a short distance, then ascends about 0.25 mile along a relatively steep bluff through a stand of bur oak trees to a high plateau. After breaking free from the trees, the trail follows this plateau of grasses and flowers, then descends to a fence used for bison management. The park provides a gate in the fence to access the trail. From here you descend a short distance along the trail to where you must ford Flynn Creek, which offers an excellent example of riparian habitat. From here the trail ascends again, passing through stands of bur oak, which is the only oak indigenous to the Black Hills. As the trail reaches the next plateau, Hay Flats, the path winds through stands of ponderosa pine on the edge of the flats. The trail follows the plateau, simultaneously passing numerous bison wallows. Soon the trail encounters another bison fence, again with a gate provided. The fences divide the park into smaller pasturelike divisions so that the bison can be rotated among them, thus not overgrazing any one area. About 3 miles out, the trail concludes where it began, by Lame Johnny Creek.

Hikes in South Dakota
Harney Range

Black Elk, a prominent medicine man among the Oglala people, considered Harney Peak the center of the world. For him, it was a place for vision quests and spiritual rejuvenation. Harney Peak is also significant because it is the highest peak east of the main chain of the Rocky Mountains.

Harney Peak's features enchant hikers who follow trails to the peak's 7,242-foot summit. From a historic lookout tower atop the summit, hikers have distant panoramic views of South Dakota, Nebraska, Wyoming, and Montana, as well as close-up vantage points of the granite formations and cliffs of the Black Elk Wilderness.

Because of its historical, geological, and spiritual significance, this high, craggy granite peak is home to many trails. Each route threads through different terrain. Each season is different, too, and in years of light snowfall, the trails are accessible year-round. The Black Elk Wilderness area in the Harney Range is a fragile place, protected by the Black Hills National Forest, and a free, self-registration form is needed (available at trailheads) if you're going to hike here. Restrictions regarding the Black Elk Wilderness are printed on the form. Be sure to follow the instructions; you'll be helping to preserve a beautiful, important part of the Black Hills.

13 Willow Creek Loop

An easy loop trail with periodic vistas of Harney Peak.

Start: From the Willow Creek Horse Camp on South Dakota Highway 244.
Distance: 1.5-mile loop.
Approximate hiking time: 1½ to 2 hours.
Difficulty: Easy.
Seasons: Best in spring through fall.
Other trail users: Heavy horse use.

Maps: National Geographic/ Trails Illustrated Topo Map No. 238; Black Hills National Forest Map; USGS Hill City and Custer quads.
Trail contact: Black Hills National Forest Supervisor's Office and Visitor Center, RR 2, Box 200, Custer, SD 57730, (605) 673-2251, www.theblack hills.com.

Finding the trailhead: The trailhead is located at Willow Creek Horse Camp on SD 244, about 4 miles east of the turnoff onto SD 244 from U.S. Highways 16/385. From the east, Willow Creek Horse Camp is about 4 miles west of the Mount Rushmore Memorial on SD 244 (Opposite Palmer Creek KOA).

The Hike

Willow Creek Loop Trail provides vistas of Harney Peak, a bird's-eye view of the spires of Elkhorn Mountain, and a stroll through stands of some of the Black Hills' largest ponderosa pines. Starting from Willow Creek Horse Camp, proceed south–southwest (counterclockwise) on Trails #2 and #8. Along the way short spur trails lead from the main trail. One short spur takes hikers to a small dam on Willow Creek. Depending on the season and the year, Willow Creek can be a full flow or a quiet seep.

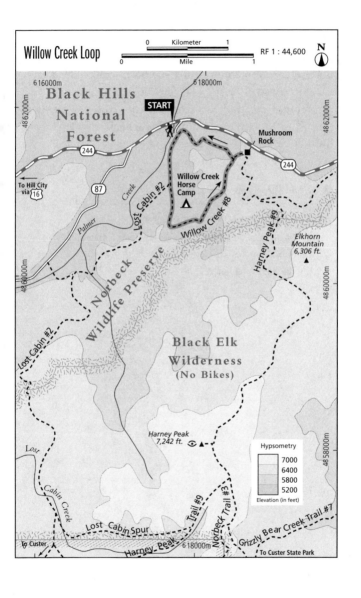

Willow Creek Loop

Kilometer

Mile

RF 1 : 44,600

N

Black Hills National Forest

START

244

To Hill City via 16

87

Palmer Creek

Lost Cabin #2

Willow Creek Horse Camp

Willow Creek #8

Mushroom Rock

244

Harney Peak #9

Elkhorn Mountain 6,306 ft.

Norbeck Wildlife Preserve

Lost Cabin #2

Black Elk Wilderness (No Bikes)

Harney Peak 7,242 ft.

Lost

Cabin Creek

To Custer

Lost Cabin Spur

Harney Peak Trail #9

Norbeck Trail #3

Grizzly Bear Creek Trail #7

To Custer State Park

Hypsometry	
	7000
	6400
	5800
	5200

Elevation (in feet)

About 1 mile from the trailhead (about two-thirds of the way around the loop), a 600-foot-long spur trail ascends to Mushroom Rock. Here, hikers are offered views of Harney Peak and the spires of Elkhorn Mountain. Mushroom Rock is a large rock outcropping that has been sculpted by weathering into a shape that could only be named as it is.

Because the trail access is directly across the highway from a KOA campground, this loop hike provides exceptional access for KOA campers and for those camped at the Willow Creek Campground.

Miles and Directions

0.0   Begin at Willow Creek Horse Camp.

1.0   Hiking counterclockwise, you'll encounter a spur trail to Mushroom Rock.

1.5   The loop is complete.

14 Iron Mountain Loop

A loop hike from mountaintop to forest floor while threading over streams, into small valleys flanked by rock formations, and through parklike settings cut by beaver dams.

Start: From the Iron Mountain Picnic Area on Iron Mountain Road.
Distance: 5.1-mile loop.
Approximate hiking time: 4 hours.
Difficulty: Easy to moderate.
Seasons: May through October.
Other trail users: Horses.
Fees and permits: Free Black Elk Wilderness Use registration form required; the panel with forms is located directly west of the parking area.
Maps: National Geographic/ Trails Illustrated Topo Map No. 238; Black Hills National Forest Map: USGS Hill City and Custer quads.
Trail contact: Black Hills National Forest Supervisor's Office and Visitor Center, RR 2, Box 200, Custer, SD 57730, (605) 673-2251, www.theblack hills.com.

Finding the trailhead: From Peter Norbeck Visitor Center in Custer State Park, take U.S. Highway 16A east for 1 mile. Take the left fork at the sign for Iron Mountain Road and follow that for 2 miles. Take a left onto Iron Mountain Road (US 16A) toward Mount Rushmore for 12.9 miles to the trailhead sign on the left (you're in the Peter Norbeck Wildlife Preserve). The trail begins at the west end of the parking area of the Iron Mountain picnic area.

The Hike

The Iron Mountain Trail is a hike providing glimpses of many facets of the Black Hills. You'll see fascinating rock

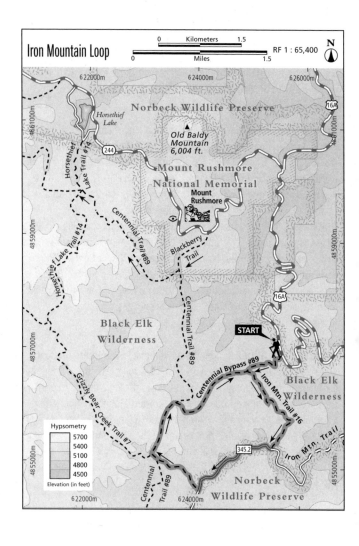

Iron Mountain Loop

Kilometers
0   1.5
Miles
0   1.5

RF 1 : 65,400

N

Norbeck Wildlife Preserve

Horsethief Lake

▲ Old Baldy Mountain 6,004 ft.

Mount Rushmore National Memorial

Mount Rushmore

244

Horsethief Lake Trail #14

Centennial Trail #89

Blackberry Trail

Centennial Trail #89

16A

Black Elk Wilderness

Grizzly Bear Creek Trail #7

START

Centennial Bypass #89

Iron Mtn. Trail #16

Black Elk Wilderness

Iron Mtn. Trail

345.2

Hypsometry
5700
5400
5100
4800
4500
Elevation (in feet)

Centennial Trail #89

Norbeck Wildlife Preserve

formations within the first mile. You'll cross Iron Creek several times as the trail meanders through the mountains. You'll be treated to more rock formations and small wildlife. We caught a glimpse of an elusive mink. If you're hiking in the fall, the leaf colors intermingle with the dark green of the ponderosa pines, lending even more drama to the igneous rock. The hike is easy to moderate, taking up to four hours, and provides a peaceful, beautiful trek.

Entirely within the Black Elk Wilderness, the trail is open in most parts to horseback riders, but *not* to bike riders.

The trail begins as a wide dirt trail blazed "#89B." It heads west for 0.5 mile, then joins the Iron Mountain Trail #16, going south (left). Along here look for a unique rock shaped like a turtle. After 1.7 miles you'll intersect with an improved gravel road, Forest Road 345, and here you turn right onto the road in a southwest direction. Follow the road for about 1 mile, crossing five bridges over Iron Creek. Take the next trail to your right (northwest); the sign says GRIZZLY BEAR CREEK #7, CENTENNIAL TRAIL #89, AND HARNEY PEAK. After about 0.5 mile, the trail takes a hard right (the sign indicates CENTENNIAL TRAIL #89) and heads north for 0.75 of a mile, where you'll encounter yet another junction. Take Trail #89B (Centennial Bypass) to the right (northeast) for 1.2 miles, thus completing the loop.

Miles and Directions

0.0   Access the Iron Mountain Picnic Area trailhead from the asphalt path past the toilets. The trail is blazed #89B (to the west).

0.5   Go south (left) on Iron Mountain Trail #16 at the junction.

1.7   Go (southwest) right on Forest Road 345.

2.7 Take Grizzly Bear Creek Trail #7 west (right).

3.2 Take Centennial Trail #89 north (right) at the junction.

3.9 Take Centennial Bypass 89B to the east (right) at the junction.

5.1 Return to the Iron Mountain Picnic Area trailhead.

Hikes in South Dakota
Deerfield Area

n 1874, two years before the infamous Battle of the Little Bighorn, Lt. Col. George A. Custer led his army troops into the Black Hills, looking for a site that might be appropriate for constructing a fort. The area was soon mapped and settlers followed. Gold was discovered and skirmishes with the Native Americans ensued. The "hills" had been discovered.

During this early expedition, Custer and his men camped on Castle Creek at what eventually became known as Deerfield. About the same time, other mining towns also evolved, and several still linger along the route traversed by the modern Deerfield Trail, completed in 1992. A slice of history unique to the Black Hills is exposed along this trail. Some of South Dakota's best fishing is found in this area.

If one were to hike the entire Deerfield Trail, the trek should probably be a three-day outing. To whet your curiosity, we have included here an easy trail and two places to make really quick hikes. Purchase a Black Hills National Forest Map to see if any other trails seem suitable for you.

Hill City, South Dakota, "The Heart of the Hills," may be used as the jumping-off place for roads to the various Deerfield trails. Hill City is about 28 miles southwest of Rapid City on U.S. Highway 16W. To reach Hill City from Custer, take U.S. Highways 385 and 16 north for 14 miles.

15 **Spring Creek Loop**

The trail winds through woods on a ridge above Spring Creek and can be hiked on its own or as part of the Flume Trail.

Start: At the Boulder Hill trailhead on Forest Road 358, about 13.5 miles from Hill City.
Distance: 3-mile loop.
Approximate hiking time: 2 to 4 hours.
Difficulty: Easy and flat.
Seasons: Best from late spring through fall.
Maps: Black Hills National Forest Map, available for purchase at Forest Service offices and at visitor centers; USDA Forest Service Map No. 50 (Flume Trail), free at Forest Service offices and Black Hills visitor centers.
Trail contact: Mystic Ranger District, Harney Office, 23939 Highway 385, Hill City, SD 57745, (605) 574-2534.

Finding the trailhead: Spring Creek Loop Trail is accessed from the Boulder Hill trailhead, considered the midsection of the Flume Trail. From Hill City take U.S. Highway 16 east for 11.1 miles to FR 358 on the left of the highway. Follow this dirt road for 2.3 miles to the trailhead.

The Hike

Part of the Flume Creek Recreation Trail, Spring Creek Loop is marked by the distinctive red, white, and blue NRT markers on posts for the first 2 miles. The path is marked for foot travel only.

From the trailhead parking lot, we hiked counterclockwise, following the sign for Spring Creek Loop to the north. The trail immediately parallels an old road that is obviously

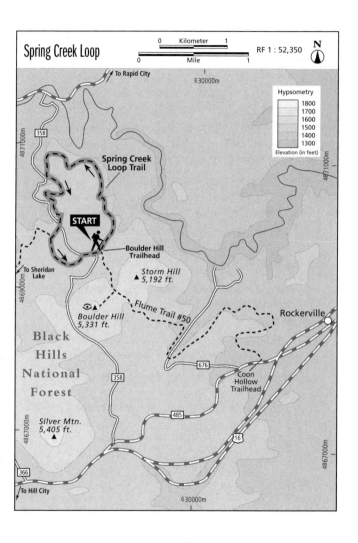

Spring Creek Loop

RF 1 : 52,350

0   Kilometer   1

0   Mile   1

N

To Rapid City

630000m

358

Spring Creek
Loop Trail

Hypsometry

1800
1700
1600
1500
1400
1300

Elevation (in feet)

START

Boulder Hill
Trailhead

Storm Hill
▲ 5,192 ft.

To Sheridan
Lake

Boulder Hill
5,331 ft.

Flume Trail #50

Rockerville

Black

Hills

National

Forest

358

676

Coon
Hollow
Trailhead

485

Silver Mtn.
5,405 ft.

16

366

To Hill City

630000m

4871000m

4869000m

4867000m

4871000m

4867000m

intended to be returned to a natural condition. A comfortable path, the trail meanders along a cliff edge and through stands of ponderosa pine.

At about 1 mile an interpretive sign informs you that you're standing on an old flume bed, 300 feet above Spring Creek. This is a great trout stream but too difficult to reach from this trail. Parallel the creek—which is more heard than seen—for 0.5 mile. The trail then begins to wind south.

Hike another 0.5 mile and you'll see rocky and woody remnants of the old flume. Here the trail becomes a bit indistinct. Continue walking south, following signs that say FOOT TRAVEL ONLY, and you will soon cross the dirt FR 358. The trail parallels the road for several hundred yards, crosses FR 358 once more, and then returns to the trailhead.

Miles and Directions

- **0.0** Start at the Boulder Hill trailhead. Head north in a counterclockwise direction.
- **1.0** You'll come to an interpretive sign.
- **2.5** Cross FR 358.
- **2.6** Cross back over FR 358.
- **3.0** The loop ends back at the Boulder Hill trailhead.

Note: If you now feel energized, consider taking a short hike on the Flume Trail in either direction from Spring Creek trailhead.

Honorable Mentions

Veterans Point Trail

Those who seek views and easy walking can take the barrier-free, 0.5-mile Veterans Point Trail around a point overlooking Pactola Reservoir. The paved walk is open all year. There is also a short one-way spur trail of 1,200 feet off the loop. The grade on the trail is 6 percent, which can be somewhat challenging for visitors using wheelchairs. However, there are curbs and railings along the trail. The path loops around a point, offering wonderful views of Pactola Reservoir, the rocky shoreline, and the hills surrounding the area.

To reach the trailhead from Hill City, take U.S. Highway 385 north for approximately 16 miles to Pactola Visitor Center. Veterans Point is located about 1 mile north of the visitor center on US 385, at the northeast end of the dam and reservoir.

Aspen Leaf Trail

This short (0.25-mile) interpretive trail was designed to show and identify several regional species of plants and trees. The first portion is barrier-free, but overall the difficulty ranges from easy to somewhat strenuous. The trail begins as a paved observation sidewalk that goes around the backside of the Pactola Visitor Center, with views of Pactola Reservoir. The trail then leads downhill on a series of steps to an obervation deck. From here, visitors can proceed downhill even farther to the edge of the reservoir.

To reach the Pactola Visitor Center, drive 16 miles north of Hill City on U.S. Highway 385.

Hikes in South Dakota
Wind Cave
National Park

Wind Cave dates back 320 million years, making it one of the world's oldest caves. The cave system contains fascinating and rare formations of Paha Sapa limestone. These formations were created by the action of water on soft rock over millions of years. The waters did not flow through but sat stagnant, dissolving Wind Cave's limestone into many passageways. In the hundred-plus years since the cave's discovery, spelunkers have explored and mapped more than 117 miles of the cave's complex system—maybe 5 percent of the total.

Park visitors can also explore Wind Cave above the ground in one of the nation's most lush and pristine prairie grasslands. Here exists an incredible prairie ecosystem and ponderosa-pine forest that host a diverse mix of wildlife throughout the park's 28,295 acres. Because motorized vehicles and mountain bikes are confined to the park's roads, hikers on the park's 30 miles of trails are generally rewarded with unparalleled sightings of wildlife. We suggest a guided cave tour below ground and three representative above-ground hikes in this wonderful national treasure.

Wind Cave National Park is just south of Custer State Park and 1¾ hours south of Rapid City.

16 Garden of Eden Cave Tour

Inside Wind Cave, viewers are presented with sights of rare beauty. The cave system has one of the largest displays of "boxwork" formations, a fragile latticework made of calcite that adorns the walls and ceilings. Other rare formations contained in the cave include "frostwork" and "helictite bushes," whose names are suggestive of their looks. The cave contains but few stalactites and stalagmites.

Recognizing the cave's extraordinary features, as well as the extraordinarily beautiful prairie ecosystem above, Congress sought protection of the Wind Cave complex. In 1903 Wind Cave became our seventh national park.

Between Memorial Day and Labor Day, the park offers three guided tours; tour prices range from $6.00 to $8.00 for adults and $3.00 to $4.00 for children ages six to sixteen. In essence, the tours are short subterranean hikes, all of which depart from the visitor center. Of the below-ground hikes, two (the Fairgrounds and the Natural Entrance Tours) are 0.5 mile in length. A third, the Garden of Eden, is 0.25 mile. These tours vary from 1 to 1½ hours each.

After Labor Day the number of tours is reduced to one, the Garden of Eden Tour, which is conducted three times daily and lasts about an hour. An elevator plummets (or so it seems) 110 feet (the equivalent of 11 stories) into the cave's depths. The water table is located many more feet down at 430 feet, or 43 stories.

Visitors on the Garden of Eden Cave Tour step from the elevator into a natural cavern, with tunnels leading off in many directions. The temperature is a constant 53 degrees throughout the cave, and the humidity varies between 90 and 100 percent.

The interpretive tour generally offers three stops, where visitors can view the "popcorn" formations as well as the rare and fragile "boxwork." Walls and formations must not be touched as oils from skin can damage them.

For added fun, the guide usually shuts off the interior electricity, and although forewarned, many are rendered speechless. An unearthly quiet cloaks the group, and a darkness blacker than any night descends. At last (after maybe sixty seconds, varying with each tour) the guide strikes a match and lights a candle lantern made from an old lard bucket. Everyone gasps. The demonstration suggests how early cave explorers found their way through the mazes. Visitors can experience the eeriness of a cave suddenly thrust into absolute darkness. No other blackness can compare.

The tour is well suited for families. It is fun, informative, and offers glimpses of the incredible beauty that is Wind Cave—below the ground.

Aboveground Hikes

Wind Cave National Park has been designated an "indicator park." Researchers here are evaluating the past effects that climate and fire have played on grassland ecology. Look for the small fenced tracts intended to exclude bison, elk, deer, and pronghorn antelope. In this system lie 28,295 acres of mixed-grass prairie and ponderosa-pine forest.

The eleven maintained trails in Wind Cave are all named; three of them are interpretive self-guided trails. The park charges no entrance fee. The elevation gain is generally minimal. All trails expose hikers to the prairie ecosystem, and hikers can combine several trails to make nice, workable loops. Several people we met had hiked all of the trails and now return summer after summer to do so again!

To get you started, we include three here that provide an introduction to grassland ecology, which in turn places you in touch with the incredible array of wildlife Wind Cave still enjoys. National Geographic/Trails Illustrated Topo Map No. 238 contains all park trails. Remember to carry lots of water, sun protection, and rain gear; always keep an eye out for snakes (although in all our time here, we never saw one) and free-roaming bison. Never attempt to approach wildlife in the park.

17 Elk Mountain Interpretive Trail

A fun, short, informative hike, suitable for the entire family.

Start: From the trailhead at the Elk Mountain Campground.
Distance: 1.2-mile loop.
Approximate hiking time: 1 to 2 hours.
Difficulty: Easy.

Seasons: Best from spring through fall.
Maps: Interpretive booklet available at the visitor center and at the trailhead.

Finding the trailhead: Readily accessible, the trail is located at the Elk Mountain Campground (the only designated campground in WCNP), which in turn is located 1.24 miles northwest from the visitor

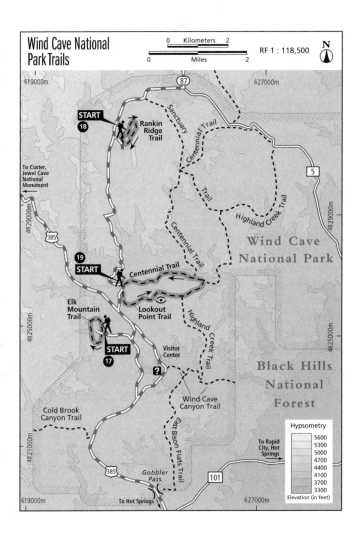

Wind Cave National Park Trails

Kilometers
0 _____ 2

Miles
0 _____ 2

RF 1 : 118,500

N

619000m

87

627000m

START
18

Rankin Ridge Trail

Sanctuary Trail

Centennial Trail

5

To Custer, Jewel Cave National Monument

4829000m

385

Centennial Trail

Highland Creek Trail

4829000m

Wind Cave National Park

19
START

Centennial Trail

4825000m

Elk Mountain Trail

Lookout Point Trail

Highland Creek Trail

START
17

Visitor Center

?

4825000m

Black Hills National Forest

Cold Brook Canyon Trail

Wind Cave Canyon Trail

Hypsometry
5600
5300
5000
4700
4400
4100
3700
3300

4821000m

385

Gobbler Pass

Beaver Flats Trail

101

To Rapid City, Hot Springs

Elevation (in feet)

619000m

627000m

To Hot Springs

center on U.S. Highway 385. The trailhead is opposite the camp-ground outdoor amphitheater.

The Hike

The path winds slightly upwards, then proceeds through a prairie environment. It then enters into the ponderosa-pine forest, where reminders of a 1991 wildfire linger. An interpretive booklet that further enhances the walk is available at the trailhead or from the visitor center.

18 Rankin Ridge Interpretive Trail

A trail wandering through ponderosa-pine forest, providing vistas of the park and its immense surroundings.

See map on page 57.
Start: From the parking lot of the Rankin Ridge Fire Tower.
Distance: 1-mile loop.
Approximate hiking time: 1 hour.
Difficulty: Moderate.
Seasons: Best from late spring through fall.

Maps: National Geographic/ Trails Illustrated Topo map No. 238; interpretive brochure available at the visitor center.
Trail contact: Wind Cave National Park, RR 1, Box 190, Hot Springs, SD 57747, (605) 745-4600, www.nps.gov/wica.

Finding the trailhead: Take U.S. Highway 385 north from the visitor center to South Dakota Highway 87 north. Take SD 87 north for about 4 miles to the sign and the road for the fire tower, which is on the right. The trailhead is located in the fire tower's parking lot.

The Hike

The trail provides a delightful climb up Rankin Ridge, offering sweeping views of the park and beyond. From the ridge the view suggests immense geological phenomena to the east. Red Valley cuts a spectacular swath through the foreground while the Hog Back Ridge, with its Bison Gap, suggests a ring engulfing the Black Hills. The White River Badlands, once a part of the Black Hills, shimmer in the distance. The trail is well interpreted, and the park provides a booklet (available at the trailhead and visitor center) for the fourteen interpreted stops.

Following the park's suggested route, the trail begins on a more northerly aspect than its southern terminus, both of which are accessed from the parking lot. The trail ascends quickly, entering a prime example of a previous prescribed burn of ponderosa pines, which are so dominant they would soon crowd out the adjacent grasslands. Along the way, several log benches provide opportunities to rest and further explore the panorama sweeping before you. Bring your binoculars.

Approximately 0.5 mile from the trailhead, you reach the fire tower, elevation 5,013 feet. For the brave and hardy, 72 steps climb to the observation deck. Look west toward the heart of the Black Hills; the ancient updoming effect is apparent.

The 0.5-mile descent on a dirt road passes through a ponderosa-pine forest and returns you to the parking lot.

19 Lookout Point-Centennial Trail Loop

A loop hike giving you a chance to examine both prairie and riparian habitats.

See map on page 57.
Start: From the Lookout Point/Centennial Trail trailhead on South Dakota Highway 87.
Distance: 4-mile loop.
Approximate hiking time: 2 to 4 hours.
Difficulty: Easy.
Seasons: April through October.

Maps: National Geographic/Trails Illustrated Topo Map No. 238; free park map and brochure available at the visitor center.
Trail contact: Wind Cave National Park, RR 1, Box 190, Hot Springs, SD 57747, (605) 745–4600, www.nps.gov/wica.

Finding the trailhead: From the visitor center, drive north for 1.75 miles on U.S. Highway 385 until it intersects with SD 87. Continue 0.62 mile along the road to the Lookout Point/Centennial Trail trailhead (they are one and the same), which is marked distinctly.

The Hike

Few trails in the Black Hills offer the opportunity to view both a pristine prairie and riparian ecosystem. Though the trail is easy, with only a few ascents and descents, some hikers may at times categorize the trail as moderate, but only because of the eight stream crossings, five of which must sometimes be made without the help of logs. Park rangers have placed logs flattened on top at several locations, which serve to facilitate crossings.

The trail begins by gently rising onto a tallgrass prairie ecosystem, characterized by a variety of grasses and, in summer, by a beautiful progression of wildflowers. After 1 mile of easy walking, the trail reaches its zenith at Lookout Point, elevation 4,480 feet. The trail does not lead directly to Lookout Point, but that is just a short jaunt to your right. From here the trail gently descends and cuts through the northern end of Prairie Dog Canyon. Abundant evidence exists demonstrating just how these small rodents, when acting in concert, can drastically alter the prairie to meet their own requirements. Because prairie dogs must rely for survival on defensive strategies, they have cut the grass to improve their vistas. In so doing, these changes attract other commonly seen wildlife species, such as the bison, coyote, and rattlesnake. Be forewarned!

The trail joins with the Highland Creek Trail 0.9 mile later, at which point hikers should turn left or backtrack on the Lookout Point Trail. If you elect to complete the loop, 2.1 miles of walking remain.

From the junction the trail descends 200 feet to Beaver Creek. As it does, the vegetation changes abruptly to ponderosa pine, the invader. If not checked, ponderosa would soon encroach beyond its historic boundaries and take over much of the prairie. Prescribed burns, conducted in the spring and fall, curtail its growth.

From Beaver Creek proceed west. One-eighth mile later, just before it joins the Centennial Trail (#89 to the west), the trail crosses the creek and then does so again on four different occasions. To avoid wet feet, crossings may require imagination and enterprise, particularly following heavy rains.

The hike along Beaver Creek offers views of varied colored rock bluffs, some a brilliant orange. High caves cut into the bluffs, and trees that have somehow established a toehold stand as sentinels at the entrances to some of these high-rock cuts. Along the stream proper, boot prints of hikers mingle with those of bison and deer, and it is not uncommon to see either.

As the trail nears its end, waters from Cold Spring Creek merge with those of Beaver Creek, which continues its eastern trend. Near the terminus, the trail ascends and shortly concludes at the Centennial Trail trailhead.

Miles and Directions

0.0   Start at the Lookout Point/Centennial Trail trailhead.

1.0   The trail reaches it highest elevation, Lookout Point.

2.0   Reach the Lookout Point/Highland Creek Trail junction on the right. Stay left (northeast).

2.3   Go left (west) at the junction with the Centennial Trail.

4.0   The loop ends at the Centennial trailhead.

Hikes in South Dakota

Badlands
National Park

The Lakota people call the Badlands Mako Sica, which means "land that is bad." Millions of years ago oceans covered this land, depositing sediments. Then came volcanic activity and the updoming of the Black Hills. Only the most hardened sandstones remain: Some appear as great castles and pyramids, others as fluted spires and mushroom shapes. Here, too, were the fossilized remains of three-toed horses, prehistoric rhinos and pigs, saber-toothed cats, and sea life.

Today hikers are fortunate to have numerous trails coursing through 244,000 acres, 64,000 of which are wilderness. Most hikes in the Badlands are easy, so we've chosen four hikes that offer great interest and at times—particularly in the early morning and late evening—extraordinary beauty.

Badlands National Park is located in southwestern South Dakota, about 70 miles east of the Black Hills. It is bordered on the southeast side by the Pine Ridge Indian Reservation. The entrance and the Ben Reifel Visitor Center are 83 miles east of Rapid City off Interstate 90 (exit 109). Cedar Pass and Sage Creek Primitive Campgrounds, are open all year on a first-come, first-served basis. Dogs are not allowed on trails and must be leashed on roads and in campgrounds.

20–22 The Door, Window, and Notch Trails

We have placed these three short hikes together as they all depart from the same trailhead. On these journeys hikers can view some of the park's most rugged rock formations.

Start: At the parking lot 2 miles east of the Ben Reifel Visitor Center.
Distances: All out and back: Door, 0.75 mile; Window, 0.25 mile; Notch, 1.5 miles.
Difficulty: Easy for Door and Window Trails; easy to moderate for Notch Trail.

Seasons: Best from spring through fall.
Maps: Small brown posts assist you on the Door and Notch Trails.
Trail Contacts: Badlands National Park, PO Box 6, Interior, SD 57750-0006, (605) 433-5361, www.badlands.national-park.com.

Finding the trailhead: The trails are accessible from a parking lot 2 miles east of the Ben Reifel Visitor Center, along Badlands Loop Road 240.

The Hikes

The first 100 yards of the **Door Trail** are barrier-free and allow one to enter and pass through the "door," where some of the area's most rugged terrain greets you. The rest of the trail is rough but flat, and sturdy shoes are recommended. If you go off-trail, the terrain is fragile and many edges are loose. Exercise caution!

Throughout the area hikers are treated to vast panoramas of spires, "doors in the walls," and steep gullies. Because of

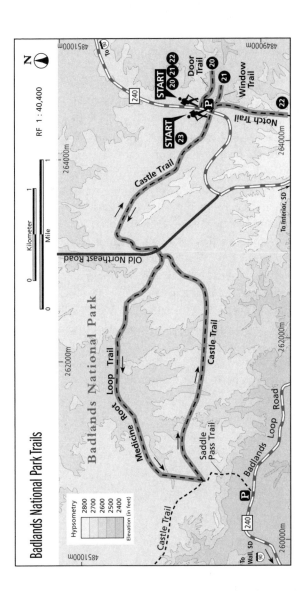

Badlands National Park Trails

the interplay of light, the design changes constantly, almost whimsically, creating a photographer's paradise, especially in the morning and early evening. Nothing here is ever the same. Small brown markers denote the route.

Window Trail is an easy 0.25-mile walk to a natural "window" in the Badlands Wall, through which visitors can peek at a stupendous view of the eroded canyon. This trail is also barrier-free, though trail conditions can be a bit rough.

Notch Trail is a hike of great beauty, but one not recommended to those with a fear of heights. For the first 0.25 mile, the path meanders through the canyon floor—around rocks and delicate prairie flowers—until it reaches a sixty-one-rung ladder, which is cabled into the hill. Here is where those afraid of heights might want to turn back. Upon reaching the top of the ladder, the scuffed trail winds around rock ledges above the canyon for about 0.5 mile until it emerges and ends at the top of a cliff, providing a commanding overlook of the White River Valley and Pine Ridge. Here, you stand on part of a cliff that collapsed long ago and formed the Cliff Shelf Nature Trail, lying directly below. *Caution:* This trail can be dangerously slippery when wet. Brown posts mark the route.

23 Castle Trail and Medicine Root Loop

Wonderful photo opportunities await as this trail wanders through the grasslands, offering views of the jagged Wall formations.

See map on page 65.
Start: Across the road from the parking lot 2 miles east of the Ben Reifel Visitor Center.
Distance: 5.0-mile lollipop.
Approximate hiking time: 2 to 4 hours.
Difficulty: Easy to moderate.
Season: Best from spring through fall.

Maps: National Geographic/ Trails Illustrated Topo Map No. 239; guide pamphlets and interpretive books available at the visitor centers.
Trail contact: Badlands National Park, PO Box 6, Interior, SD 57750-0006, (605) 433-5361, www.badlands.national-park.com.

Finding the trailhead: Take South Dakota Highway 240 (Badlands Loop Road) northeast from the Ben Reifel Visitor Center for approximately 2 miles to the trail parking lot on your right. The Castle Trail trailhead is across the road from the Door, Window, and Notch Trails.

The Hike

Begin your hike on the Castle Trail in a northwest direction. Follow the trail for about 0.75 mile. Just after crossing the Old Northeast Road, the Medicine Root Loop Trail comes in from your right. Leave the Castle Trail at this point and follow the Medicine Loop Trail.

Now the trail is a flat, easy walk along a narrow dirt path through the grassland area just north of the Castle Trail. As one walks along this plateau, grasslands sweep to the north while the jagged Wall formations rise to the south. Other formations range from short, flat, sod-covered "tables" to lofty spires. The area surrounding the trail is covered with cactus. Grasses hide desert wildflowers. Metal posts are abundant and serve to distinguish the trail from game paths.

Medicine Root derives its name from the numerous plants that were once used here by Native Americans. Photo opportunities abound throughout.

Medicine Root ends at the junction of Saddle Pass and Castle Trail. To complete the loop, follow the Castle Trail sign leading east (to your left). From this point the trail ambles along the base of the rock formations. The level trail is somewhat rocky but soon becomes a one-person dirt path. After a mile or so, you will once again cross the Old Northeast Road and soon be back to your vehicle.

We should mention another option: If you have two vehicles, the mostly level Castle Trail, which does not have heavy traffic, can be hiked for its full 5 miles. You could begin at either the west or east end. The trail stretches from the Door/Window parking area to the Fossil Exhibit Trail on the Badlands Loop Road.

Hikes in South Dakota
A Bit Harder

We thought we'd include these three more-challenging hikes for your consideration for several reasons. First, we feel these are among the most beautiful hikes in the different areas, especially the trip to Harney Peak. Secondly, we have seen children on all of these trails (tired, but still going!). And last, perhaps the "easy trails" didn't offer quite enough challenge for some of you.

24 Crow Peak Trail #64, Spearfish Area

We've selected this one because it provides excellent panoramic views, and because we talked to several families with children who said that because of the sweeping views, the trail rated high with them.

Start: From the trailhead parking lot on Forest Road 214, about 6.9 miles west of Spearfish, South Dakota.

Distance: 7 miles out and back.

Approximate hiking time: Most of a day.

Difficulty: Moderately strenuous to strenuous.

Elevation gain: 1,560 feet.

Seasons: Late spring through fall.

Maps: Black Hills National Forest Map; USDA FS Crow Peak Trail Map #64 and Black Hills National Forest eight-page handout of Spearfish Trails, free and available at Forest Service offices and visitor centers.

Trail contact: Northern Hills Ranger District, 2014 North Main, Spearfish, SD 57783, (605) 642–4622.

Finding the trailhead: The trailhead is located 6.9 miles west of Spearfish, South Dakota (off Interstate 90, exit 10). Take Utah Street (1 block east of the Forest Service Office) west for 2.6 miles past a four-way stop sign. Take a left on Higgins Gulch Road (FR 214, a good gravel road) and follow it for 3.9 miles to the trailhead, located at a large parking area on the right.

The Hike

Crow Peak Trail is a popular hike. The trail winds up to the mountain's top, providing sweeping vistas at the summit. Crow Peak is so named because of a battle once fought here between the Crow and Sioux Indians. Appropriately, the

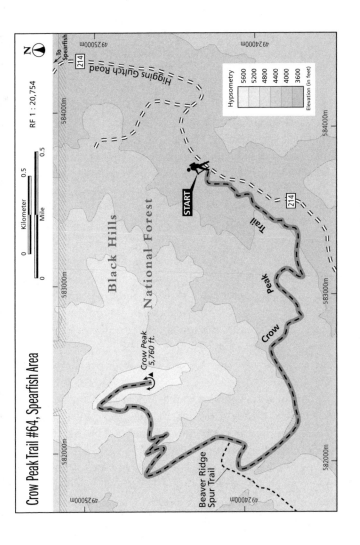

Crow Peak Trail #64, Spearfish Area

RF 1 : 20,754

Kilometer

Mile

Black Hills

National Forest

START

Crow Peak
5,760 ft.

Crow Peak Trail

214

Beaver Ridge
Spur Trail

To Spearfish

Higgins Gulch Road

214

Hypsometry

5600
5200
4800
4400
4000
3600

Elevation (in feet)

mountain in Sioux tongue, Paha Karitukateyapi, translates to "the place where the Sioux killed the Crow."

Crow Peak is an igneous intrusion and was formed in the same manner as Bear Butte and several other peaks in the area. Eons ago molten magma filled limestone and sedimentary layers, which then cooled to form the hard igneous rock. Erosion and washing away of sedimentary deposits continues to re-form the hills in the area.

The trail begins in Higgins Gulch amidst ponderosa-pine woods and much new growth of native bushes and bur oak. The entire 3.5-mile ascent is moderate in some places, strenuous in others. The route heads west on the southern side of the hill and climbs ever upward. The trail is well blazed on trees with one large rectangle directly below a smaller rectangle.

At about 1.5 miles hikers encounter a junction. Here you might want to take the 1-mile round-trip Beaver Ridge Spur Trail to the south for more views in a peaceful atmosphere. If not, continue in a northerly direction toward the summit.

As the trail nears the top, the forest thins and the path becomes rockier. Simultaneously the trail offers the promise of spectacular views ahead—and then at the peak lives up to its promise.

Our hike occurred on a mid-September day when several inches of early snow covered the peak. Where valleys retained pockets of cold, snow had lingered. At the summit the contrast between the valley and the peak was dramatic. Below, fall had barely tinged the trees, but several thousand feet higher, fall and winter were already colliding. The view from the top is almost surrealistic. Lookout, Spearfish, and Terry Peaks, as well as Bear Butte, among others, appear in the east. The plains of eastern Montana and the Bearlodge

Mountains of Wyoming lie to the west, with Warren Peak sometimes visible. Spread below is the town of Spearfish, nestled in all this beauty.

Crow Peak Trail is designated for hikers and horseback riders only. The trail exhibits but little evidence of horse use, and the typical erosion that often results from the trodding of heavy animals is absent. Because the trail is steep, the extra exertion may cause hikers to become dehydrated. Carry an ample supply of drinking water.

25 Bear Butte, Bear Butte State Park Area

Although Bear Butte is not part of the Black Hills proper, its inclusion is justified for several reasons. Historically, Bear Butte stood as a landmark, pointing the way for many early-day "hikers," trudging across the prairie in search of wild game, gold, furs, or homesteads in the Black Hills. Because of its prominence and beauty, the Butte has served as a beacon. It still does. Rising 1,200 feet above the plains, it is located just outside the northeast corner of the Black Hills, approximately 6 miles northeast of Sturgis, South Dakota, and is part of Bear Butte State Park. Mato Paha (Bear Mountain) is not a butte at all, but a solitary mountain formed millions of years ago. Bear Butte is the northern terminus for the Centennial Trail, which courses more than 100 miles through the Black Hills.

In 1996 a massive fire ravaged much of Bear Butte, consuming about 90 percent of the ponderosa-pine trees on the

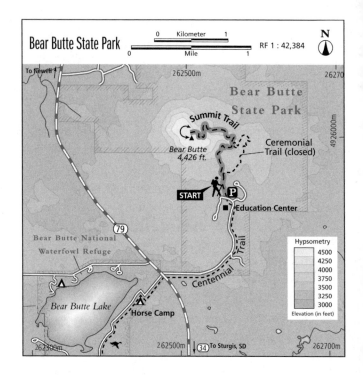

mountain. One trail, the Ceremonial Trail, is now permanently closed. The effects of the fire on the trees will remain for many, many years, but the surrounding grasslands are rebounding more quickly. The natural process of fire and its part in ecology is evidenced in a huge way as you will see on your hike.

Though the Summit Trail is not one of the easiest of the easy day hikes, it is included here because it provides such sweeping views, and because it provides a significant chapter in the history of Native Americans.

A trek from the base to the peak of a sacred mountain, the trail winds through a pine forest; many tree branches are draped with prayer flags and ceremonial objects.

Start: At the Bear Butte Education Center.

Distance: 3.6 miles out and back.

Approximate hiking time: 2 to 3 hours.

Difficulty: Moderately strenuous to strenuous, due to the sharp ascent over a relatively short distance.

Elevation gain: 1,026 feet.

Seasons: Best from late spring through fall.

Maps: USDA FS Centennial Trail User Guide; info map available at the Bear Butte Education Center.

Trail contact: Bear Butte State Park, Box 688, Sturgis, SD 57785, (605) 347-5240.

Finding the trailhead: From Sturgis (17 miles east of Spearfish on Interstate 90, or 27 miles west of Rapid City), take South Dakota Highway 34 east for 4 miles to South Dakota Highway 79. Go north on SD 79 for 4 miles to the sign on the right for Bear Butte State Park; there is camping along the shores of Bear Butte Lake (across SD 79 from the park entrance). The trailhead is located at the Bear Butte Education Center. Another trailhead sits directly across SD 79 from the turn-in for the state park. This is the Centennial Trail, and hikers could add 1.5 miles to their hike by departing from here. For this hike we begin at the education center.

The Hike

The Bear Butte State Park Education Center explains more about the area's natural history and its significance to Native Americans. Outside the education center is a bust of Frank Fools Crow (1809-1889), the ceremonial chief of the Teton Lakota Sioux and a nephew of Black Elk, who was present as a teenager at the Battle of Little Bighorn. The park's relatively short, steep trail provides an excursion imbued with beauty and spirituality. Simultaneously the trail provides access to the top of Bear Butte, which offers unspoiled panoramic views. Bear Butte is a spiritual place for Native

Americans who come here to pray and leave offerings, so pictures should not be taken of them and offerings should not be disturbed.

Begin the hike on the Summit Trail, which is well marked at the trailhead. This trail lies to the west of the Ceremonial Trail, no longer in use since the 1996 fire.

The Summit Trail winds through pines and around the cliffs, with numerous switchbacks. Where washouts might occur, park managers have placed log steps. The lookout is

ON THE DAY of our hike, a mist shrouded the land but did not obscure the distant features. Rather, it combined with the golden leaves and served to heighten the mystery and spirituality of the area. I met Ralph Red Fox at Bear Butte on another day, in September, when snow was falling. He must have noticed the dreamcatcher hanging on the mirror in my van, since he waved at me as I stepped from the vehicle. His brown face was lined, and his head was crowded with a full crop of black hair tinged with silver. He said he was traveling home to Idaho but had stopped at Bear Butte for spiritual rejuvenation. We spoke quietly for a few moments, and then he said he would be returning in the evening for a sweat in one of the lodges below us and that I was welcome to join him.

I thanked Red Fox but told him I could not make a commitment. "The weather," I said, motioning to the falling snow covering the leaves of green and gold.

He asked me to walk with him for a moment down a trail, where he picked some sage. He rolled the fragrant leaves between his palms. Then he moved his hands in the four directions and asked me to meditate with him. Finally, Red Fox placed the sage in my left palm and crossed my right palm over the left, joining my hands. "Burn this for good luck as you travel," he said.

I thanked him but said little. I wished I had something to give him in return.

reached after 1.4 miles and hikers find themselves standing on a platform above an enormous talus slope. Hikers reach the summit 0.4 mile later and are rewarded with commanding 360-degree views of bison, ponds, farms, and cattle; of the Black Hills looming to the southwest; and of the Badlands to the east. From the peak, retrace your hike to the parking lot.

Miles and Directions

0.0 Start at the trailhead of Summit Trail, going north from the education center. The Summit Trail is shared here with the Centennial Trail.

1.0 Continue north/northwest on the Summit Trail.

1.4 A platform overlooks the talus slope, facing north.

1.8 Retrace your hike from the summit.

3.6 Return to the trailhead.

26 Sylvan Lake to Harney Peak Trail, Harney Area

A trip up the highest mountain east of the main chain of the Rocky Mountains offering varied and spectacular scenery.

Start: From the Sylvan Lake Day-Use Area in Custer State Park off South Dakota Highway 87.
Distance: 6.8 miles out and back.
Approximate hiking time: Plan on a full day.
Difficulty: Moderately difficult, with heavy summer traffic.
Elevation gain: 1,142 feet.
Seasons: From late spring through fall.
Fees and permits: Custer State

Park entry permit required when hiking from any trailheads within the park. Also, free Black Elk Wilderness Use registration form required. Available at boxes as you enter the wilderness.

Maps: Custer State Park Trail Guide, free and available at entrance stations and visitor centers; National Geographic/ Trails Illustrated Topo Map No. 238; Black Hills National Forest Map; USGS Map, Custer Quad.

Trail contact: Hell Canyon Ranger District, Custer Office, 330 Mount Rushmore Road, Custer, SD 57730, (605) 673-4853.

Finding the trailhead: Take South Dakota Highway 89N from Custer, South Dakota, for 6 miles to the Sylvan Lake Entrance Station. Follow signs to Sylvan Lake. Or from Peter Norbeck Visitor Center, take U.S. Highway 16A west to SD 87 north (the Needles Highway) to Sylvan Lake, a distance of 19 miles. Access the trail from the Sylvan Lake Day-Use Area. Follow #9 blazes on trees (which are not always distinct).

The Hike

The trail provides an easy to moderate ascent for the first mile, then descends gently to the Midway area by Lost Cabin Creek. This area has no facilities. Water from the creek should not be consumed unless purified.

During the initial ascent you'll encounter a rocky outcrop with outstanding views of Harney Peak and its surroundings. After the Midway area the trail ascends once more, reaching a ridge that is fairly flat. About 0.25 mile later Norbeck Trail #3 joins the trail. Continue to follow Trail #9 blazes on trees, now to the north (left).

The final ascent of about 1 mile is steep with several switchbacks. It is flanked by stands of ponderosa pine and granite formations; in the spring and summer wildflowers abound.

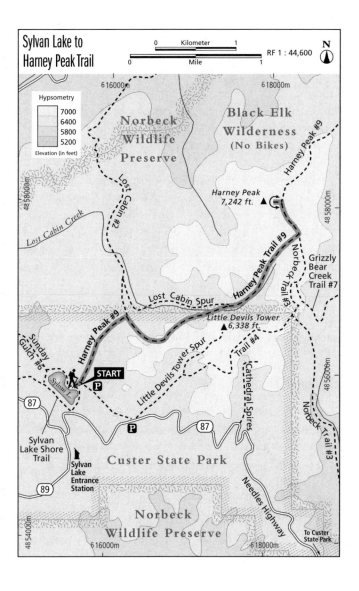

Sylvan Lake to Harney Peak Trail

Kilometer
0   1

Mile
0   1

RF 1 : 44,600

N

Hypsometry

Elevation (in feet)
7000
6400
5800
5200

616000m

618000m

Black Elk Wilderness (No Bikes)

Harney Peak #9

Norbeck Wildlife Preserve

4858000m

Lost Cabin #2

Lost Cabin Creek

Harney Peak 7,242 ft. ▲

Harney Peak Trail #9

Norbeck Trail #3

4858000m

Grizzly Bear Creek Trail #7

Lost Cabin Spur

Harney Peak #9

Little Devils Tower ▲ 6,338 ft.

Little Devils Tower Spur

Trail #4

4856000m

Sunday Gulch #6

Sylvan L.

START
P

87

Cathedral Spires

Norbeck Trail #3

P

87

Sylvan Lake Shore Trail

89

Sylvan Lake Entrance Station

Custer State Park

Needles Highway

Norbeck Wildlife Preserve

4854000m

616000m

618000m

To Custer State Park

Close to the summit the trail is sprinkled with mica. Stone and mortar steps facilitate the final climb through the rocks. Group consensus proclaims the grunt to the top is worth the effort. The views of four different states rolling off and eventually merging with the horizon are inspiring. To the north, in the not-so-great distance, looms the backside of Mount Rushmore, while to the south, at a distance of about 1 mile, rugged Little Devils Tower juts to a height of 6,338 feet.

In the immediate vicinity rock formations lace the area; the fire tower (no longer in use) straddles the most lofty of these. On clear days the life of a fire lookout ranger could be grand, but it's easy to imagine times when winds buffeted the tower and lightning threaded the drab sky or stabbed night's inky cloak, striking the tower and engulfing it with St. Elmo's fire.

Because of Harney Peak's grandeur, be prepared for crowds. Thunderstorms, particularly in July and August, are frequent and produce hail and lightning. At times, the sun blazes, so carry plenty of water, especially in summer.

Miles and Directions

- **0.0** Start at the Sylvan Lake-Harney Trail #9 trailhead.
- **0.75** Lost Cabin Trail #2 enters from north. Stay east (right) on #9.
- **1.4** Enter the Black Elk Wilderness; registration required.
- **2.6** At the intersection with Norbeck Trail #3, stay on #9 north (left).
- **3.4** Retrace your steps from Harney Peak.
- **6.8** Return to Sylvan Lake.

Hikes in South Dakota
Hike/Bike Trails

The Black Hills area boasts two long hike/bike trails. We mention them here because they are unique in many ways, and because we want you to know they exist. Perhaps you've brought your bike along and are in the mood for a short ride in one of these beautiful areas. Both trails offer many trailhead entrances and exits, thus making them also friendly for a short walk. As far as biking is concerned, the Mickelson Trail, stretching for 114 miles from Deadwood, South Dakota, in the north to Edgemont, South Dakota, in the south, is for bikers of any ability; the 111-mile-long Centennial Trail is more for adventurous, experienced mountain bikers. Twenty-four trailheads dot this latter trek and offer hikers a chance to get off the beaten path into the silence, nature, and beauty of the Black Hills. Detailed maps of both trails are available at bike shops, by calling (800) 732–5682, or e-mailing sdinfo@state.sd.us.

27 George S. Mickelson Trail

Dumont to Mystic (A Best Easy Day Bicycle Ride)

Named for South Dakota governor George Mickelson, who championed it and then met an untimely death in a 1993 plane crash, the Mickelson Trail is an abandoned railroad bed that has undergone a rails-to-trails transformation through the joint efforts of government agencies and local volunteers. Completed in the fall of 1998, the 10-foot-wide trail offers 114 miles and fourteen trailheads of scenic beauty and gentle grades (none more than 4 percent) for nonmotorized recreation between Deadwood and Edgemont. Four restored hard-rock tunnels and more than 100 railroad trestles along the Rochford-to-Mystic stretch speak to its railroading past.

Linda Sandness, who in her capacity as a coordinator for visitor services for South Dakota's Parks and Recreation Service has traveled the trail's length, says that although the entire trail is fascinating, she has a favorite section. She particularly enjoys the 18-mile section between Dumont and Mystic, in part because "it's all downhill, making it very nice for a family outing." Of course that leaves one person having to ride back uphill to retrieve the car, but generally that doesn't take much more than an hour. Or you can plan to leave a car in Mystic.

But Sandness says the area offers more than just an easy ride. She says the trail parallels a creek, and as you ride, you can hear the brook and all kinds of birds. You'll also enjoy the stretch for its rich and exciting interpretation of local history. Sandness played an integral role in creating the interpretive panels found along the way, which may, in part, help

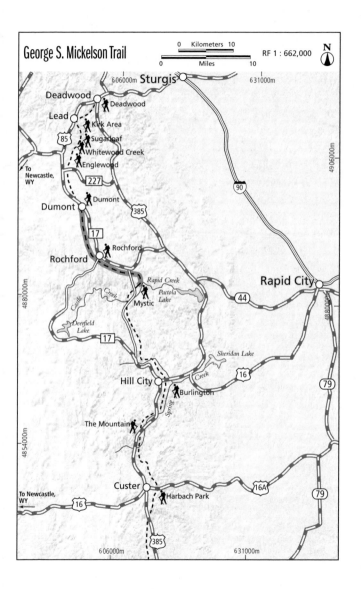

George S. Mickelson Trail

RF 1 : 662,000

Kilometers 10

Miles 10

N

Sturgis

606000m   631000m

Deadwood

Deadwood

Lead

Kirk Area

85

Sugarloaf

Whitewood Creek

Englewood

4906000m

227

90

Dumont

Dumont

385

17

Rochford

Rochford

Rapid Creek

Pactola Lake

Rapid City

4880000m

Mystic

44

Castle Creek

Deerfield Lake

17

4880000m

Sheridan Lake

Hill City

16

Burlington

79

4854000m

Spring Creek

The Mountain

To Newcastle, WY

Custer

16A

79

Harbach Park

To Newcastle, WY

16

606000m   385   631000m

explain her preference. Bottom line: She has a right to be proud, for the bike trail passes by old towns, such as Stand-off and Montana Miner, that are no longer in existence. Explaining the role they played in South Dakota's rich history has been a major department thrust, and the work required several years of planning and creation. As a result, most trailhead locations now include shelters with water and interpretive information.

This trail relies on user fees to help with its upkeep. Those twelve and older are required to buy a daily ($2.00) or annual ($10.00) trail pass. Fees are payable at self-registration boxes and some businesses along the trail. No fee is required within city limits. Call the Black Hills Trail Office for information, maps, and registration for the annual fall trail ride.

The Mickelson Trail passes through private property at some points; please respect the landowners. Pets must be leashed, and remember: Bikers yield to walkers, and everyone yields to horseback riders. The trail closes to users each day from dusk to dawn.

28 Centennial Trail

Pactola Reservoir to Sheridan Lake

The Centennial Trail has a lofty beginning and magnificent ending. If one proceeds from north to south, the trail begins at Bear Butte and Bear Butte Lake, where Crazy Horse presided over a Council of Nations. The Centennial Trail ends in Wind Cave, an area best known for its subterranean features but equally touted for its rolling prairie features that play host to a number of dramas that have their basis in grass.

The land between Bear Butte and Wind Cave is equally inspiring. Here the curtain goes up daily, for there are lakes, peaks, historic areas, and landscapes that teem with wildlife and provide hikers with endless variety. What all this boils down to is that the Centennial Trail does precisely what it was established to do: It provides hikers and horseback riders throughout (and bikers in most areas) with an opportunity to relive the fabulous history that is South Dakota and evaluate for themselves what magnificent natural treasures the state still retains.

Though the Centennial Trail can be backpacked in one grand outing, its 111 miles can also be hiked or biked segmentally. The trail provides twenty-four trailheads, conveniently located for excursions of 4 to 10 miles. As a best easy day hike/ride, we recommend the 10-mile stretch between Pactola Reservoir and Sheridan Lake. Start at the Rapid Creek Trailhead at Pactola. From South Dakota Highway 44 west of Rapid City, go 2.1 miles south on U.S. Highway 385, turn left onto gravel Pactola Basin Road, then go 0.5 mile to a four-way intersection, turn left, and park at the trailhead. Drop a second vehicle at Dakota Point Trailhead

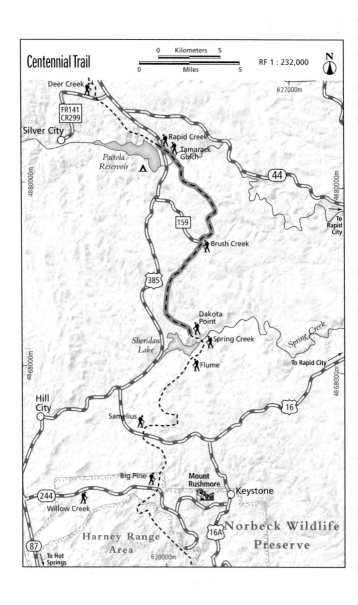

by taking US 385; go east 1.6 miles on Sheridan Lake Road southwest of Rapid City, turn right onto gravel Dakota Point Road (Forest Road 434), and go another 0.3 mile to the trailhead, which will be on your left. Obviously you can do this in the reverse if you wish.

About the Authors

Bert and Jane Gildart are self-described "wanderers," seeking out special places across the country. Together they have hiked, biked, skied, and boated hundreds of miles throughout many wilderness and backcountry areas. They also spend months each year wandering our national parks.

For thirteen summers Bert served as a backcountry ranger in Glacier National Park. He is the author of more than 400 magazine articles and eleven books.

Bert and Jane have collaborated on several FalconGuides including: *Hiking Shenandoah National Park; Best Easy Day Hikes Shenandoah; Hiking the Black Hills Country; A FalconGuide to Dinosaur National Monument;* and *A FalconGuide to Death Valley National Park.* When not off wandering, they make their home in northwest Montana, in the shadow of Glacier National Park.